The Collected Poems

of William Allingham

by

William Allingham

The Collected Poems

Table of Contents

William Allingham

William Allingham
from an early photograph

A Day-Dream's Reflection

Chequer'd with woven shadows as I lay
Among the grass, blinking the watery gleam,
I saw an Echo-Spirit in his bay
Most idly floating in the noontide beam.

Slow heaved his filmy skiff, and fell, with sway
Of ocean's giant pulsing, and the Dream,
Buoyed like the young moon on a level stream
Of greenish vapour at decline of day,

Swam airily, watching the distant flocks
Of sea-gulls, whilst a foot in careless sweep
Touched the clear-trembling cool with tiny shocks,
Faint-circling; till at last he dropt asleep,
Lull'd by the hush-song of the glittering deep,
Lap-lapping drowsily the heated rocks.

A Dream

I heard the dogs howl in the moonlight night;
I went to the window to see the sight;
All the Dead that ever I knew
Going one by one and two by two.

On they pass'd, and on they pass'd;
Townsfellows all, from first to last;

William Allingham

Born in the moonlight of the lane,
Quench'd in the heavy shadow again.

Schoolmates, marching as when they play'd
At soldiers once - but now more staid;
Those were the strangest sight to me
Who were drown'd, I knew, in the awful sea.

Straight and handsome folk, bent and weak, too;
Some that I loved, and gasp'd to speak to;
Some but a day in their churchyard bed;
Some that I had not known were dead.

A long, long crowd - where each seem'd lonely,
Yet of them all there was one, one only,
Raised a head or look'd my way;
She linger'd a moment - she might not stay.

How long since I saw that fair pale face!
Ah! Mother dear! might I only place
My head on thy breast, a moment to rest,
While thy hand on my tearful cheek were prest!

On, on, a moving bridge they made
Across the moon-stream, from shade to shade,
Young and old, women and men;
Many long-forgot, but remembered then,

And first there came a bitter laughter;
A sound of tears a moment after;
And then a music so lofty and gay,

That eve morning, day by day,
I strive to recall it if I may.

A Gravestone

Far from the churchyard dig his grave,
On some green mound beside the wave;
To westward, sea and sky alone,
And sunsets. Put a mossy stone,
With mortal name and date, a harp
And bunch of wild flowers, carven sharp;
Then leave it free to winds that blow,
And patient mosses creeping; slow,
And wandering wings, and footsteps rare
Of human creature pausing there.

A Memory

Four ducks on a pond,
A grass-bank beyond,
A blue sky of spring,
White clouds on the wing;
What a little thing
To remember for years-
To remember with tears!

William Allingham

A Seed

See how a Seed, which Autumn flung down,
And through the Winter neglected lay,
Uncoils two little green leaves and two brown,
With tiny root taking hold on the clay
As, lifting and strengthening day by day,

It pushes red branchless, sprouts new leaves,
And cell after cell the Power in it weaves
Out of the storehouse of soil and clime,
To fashion a Tree in due course of time;

Tree with rough bark and boughs' expansion,
Where the Crow can build his mansion,
Or a Man, in some new May,
Lie under whispering leaves and say,

"Are the ills of one's life so very bad
When a Green Tree makes me deliciously glad?"
As I do now. But where shall I be
When this little Seed is a tall green Tree?

A Singer

That which he did not feel, he would not sing;
What most he felt, religion it was to hide
In a dumb darkling grotto, where the spring

Of tremulous tears, arising unespied,
Became a holy well that durst not glide
Into the day with moil or murmuring;
Whereto, as if to some unlawful thing,
He stole, musing or praying at its side.

But in the sun he sang with cheerful heart,
Of coloured season and the whirling sphere,
Warm household habitude and human mirth,
The whole faith-blooded mystery of earth;
And I, who had his secret, still could hear
The grotto's whisper low through every part.

A Wife

The wife sat thoughtfully turning over
A book inscribed with the school-girl's name;
A tear, one tear, fell hot on the cover
So quickly closed when her husband came.

He came, and he went away,—it was nothing;
With commonplace words upon either side;
But, just with the sound
Of the room door shutting,
A dreadful door in her soul stood wide.

Love she had read of in sweet romances,
Love that could sorrow, but never fail;
Built her own palace of noble fancies,
All the wide world like a fairy-tale.

William Allingham

Bleak and bitter, and utterly doleful
Spread to this woman her map of life:
Hour after hour she look'd in her soul, full
Of deep dismay and turbulent strife.

Face in hands, she knelt on the carpet;
The cloud was loosen'd, the storm-rain fell.
Oh ! life has so much to wilder and warp it,
One poor heart's day what poet could tell?

Abbey Assaroe

Gray, gray is Abbey Assaroe,
By Belashanny town,
It has neither door nor window,
The walls are broken down;
The carven-stones lie scatter'd
In briar and nettle-bed!
The only feet are those that come
At burial of the dead.
A little rocky rivulet
Rruns murmuring to the tide,
Singing a song of ancient days,
In sorrow, not in pride;
The boortree and the lightsome ash
Across the portal grow,
And heaven itself is now
The roof of Abbey Assaroe.

It looks beyond the harbour-stream
To Gulban mountain blue;
It hears the voice of Erna's fall -
Atlantic breakers too;
High ships go sailing past it;
The sturdy clank of oars,
Brings in the salmon-boat to haul
A net upon the shores;
And this way to his home-creek,
When the summer day is done,
Slow sculls the weary fisherman
Across the setting sun;
While green with corn is Sheegus Hill,
His cottage white below;
But gray at every season
Is Abbey Assaroe.

There stood one day a poor old man
Above its broken bridge;
He heard no running rivulet,
He saw no mountain-ridge;
He turn'd his back on Sheegus Hill,
And view'd with misty sight
The Abbey walls, the burial-ground
With crosses ghostly white;
Under a weary weight of years
He bow'd upon his staff,
Perusing in the present time
The former's epitaph;
For, gray and wasted like the walls,

William Allingham

A figure full of woe,
This man was of the blood of them
Who founded Assaroe.

From Derry to Bundrowas Tower,
Tirconnell broad was theirs;
Spearmen and plunder, bards and wine,
And holy Abbot's prayers;
With chanting always in the house
Which they had builded high;
To God and to Saint Bernard -
Where at last they came to die.
At worst, no workhouse grave for him!
The ruins of his race
Shall rest among the ruin'd stones
Of this their saintly place.
The fond old man was weeping;
And tremulous and slow
Along the rough and crooked lane
He crept from Assaroe.

Adieu to Belshanny

Adieu to Belashanny!
Where I was bred and born;
Go where I may, I'll think of you,
As sure as night and morn.
The kindly spot, the friendly town,
Where every one is known,
And not a face in all the place

But partly seems my own;
There's not a house or window,
There's not a field or hill,
But, east or west, in foreign lands,
I recollect them still.
I leave my warm heart with you,
Tho' my back I'm forced to turn
Adieu to Belashanny,
And the winding banks of Erne!

No more on pleasant evenings
We'll saunter down the Mall,
When the trout is rising to the fly,
The salmon to the fall.
The boat comes straining on her net,
And heavily she creeps,
Cast off, cast off - she feels the oars,
And to her berth she sweeps;
Now fore and aft keep hauling,
And gathering up the clew.
Till a silver wave of salmon rolls
In among the crew.
Then they may sit, with pipes a-lit,
And many a joke and 'yarn'
Adieu to Belashanny;
And the winding banks of Erne!

The music of the waterfall,
The mirror of the tide,
When all the green-hill'd harbour is
Full from side to side,

From Portnasun to Bulliebawns,
And round the Abbey Bay,
From rocky inis saimer to
Coolnargit sand-hills gray;
While far upon the southern line,
To guard it like a wall,
The Leitrim mountains clothed in blue
Gaze calmly over all,
And watch the ship sail up or down,
The red flag at her stern
Adieu to these, adieu to all
The winding banks of Erne!

Farewell to you, Kildoney lads,
And them that pull on oar,
A lug-sail set, or haul a net,
From the Point to Mullaghmore;
From Killybegs to bold Slieve-League,
That ocean-Mountain steep,
Six hundred yards in air aloft,
Six hundred in the deep,
From Dooran to the Fairy Bridge,
And round by Tullen Strand,
Level and long, and white with waves,
Where gull and Curlew stand;
Head out to sea when on your lee
The breakers you Discern!
Adieu to all the billowy coast,
And winding banks of Erne!

Farewell, Coolmore - Bundoran!
And your summercrowds that run
From inland homes to see with joy
Th'Atlantic-setting sun;
To breathe the buoyant salted air,
And sport among the waves;
To gather shells on sandy beach,
And tempt the gloomy caves;
To watch the flowing, ebbing tide,
The boats, the crabs, The fish;
Young men and maids to meet and smile,
And form a tender wish;
The sick and old in search of health,
For all things have their turn
And I must quit my native shore,
And the winding banks of Erne!

Farewell to every white cascade
From the Harbour to Belleek
And every pool where fins may rest,
And ivy-shaded creek;
The sloping fields, the lofty rocks,
Where ash and holly grow,
The one split yew-tree gazing on
The curving flood below;
The Lough, that winds through islands
Under Turaw mountain green;
And Castle Caldwell's stretching woods,
With tranquil bays between;
And Breesie Hill, and many a pond
Among the heath and fern

For I must say adieu-adieu
To the winding banks of Erne!
The thrush will call through Camlin groves
The live- long summer day;
The waters run by mossy cliff,
And banks with wild flowers gay;
The girls will bring their work and sing
Beneath a twisted thorn,
Or stray with sweethearts down the path
Among growing corn;
Along the river-side they go,
Where I have often been,
O never shall I see again
The days that I have seen!
A thousand chances are to one
I never may return;
Adieu to Belashanny,
And the winding banks of Erne!

Adieu to evening dances,
When merry neighbours meet,
And the fiddle says to boys and girls,
"Get up shake your feet!"
To 'shanachus' and wise old talk
Of Erin's gone by -
Who trench'd the rath on such a hill,
And where the bones may lie;
Of saint, or king, or warrior chief;
With tales of fairy power,
And tender ditties sweetly sung
To pass the twilight hour.

The mournful song of exile
Is now for me to learn;
Adieu, my dear companions on
The winding banks of Erne!

Now measure from the Commons down
To each end of the Purt,
Round the Abbey, Moy, and Knather -
I wish no one any hurt;
The Main Street, Back Street, College Lane,
The Mall,and Portnasun,
If any foes of mine are there,
I pardon every one.
I hope that man and womankind
Will do the same by me;
For my heart is sore and heavy
At voyaging the sea.
My loving friends I'll bear in mind,
And often fondly turn;
To think of Belashanny,
And the winding banks of Erne.

If ever I'm a money'd man,
I mean, please God, to cast
My golden anchor in the place
Where youthful years were pass'd;
Though heads that now are black and brown
Must meanwhile gather gray,
New faces rise by every hearth,
And old ones drop away
Yet dearer still that Irish hill

Than all the world beside;
It's home, sweet home, where'er I roam,
Through lands and waters wide.
And if the Lord allows me,
I surely will return
To my native Belashanny,
And the winding banks of Erne.

Advice to a Young Poet

You're a true Poet: but, my dear,
If you would hold the public ear,
Remember to be not too clear.
Be strange, be verbally intense ;
Words matter ten times more than sense ;
In clear streams, under sunny skies,
The fish you angle for won't rise;

In turbid water, cloudy weather,
They'll rush to you by shoals together.
'Ignotum pro magnifico;'
The least part of your meaning show;
Your readers must not understand
Too well; the mist-wrapt hill looks grand,
The placid noonday mountain small.
Speak plainly, folk say—' Is that all?'

Speak riddles—' What is here? '—They read
And re-read, many times indeed;

'How fine! how strange! how deep! how new!
Here's my opinion ; what say you?
It may be this; it might be that;
Who can be certain what he's at
This necromancer ?' While they talk,
You swing your solemn cloak and stalk;
Or else look on with smile urbane,
'Well done, my children,—guess again !'

Oh, let me not advise in vain,
Be what you will, but don't be plain!
I Believe without bother
In This, That, and T'other;
Whatever is current, no matter.
I believe in Success,
And in Comfort no less;
I believe all the rest is but patter.

'Vile money !' True. Let's have enough,
To save our thinking of such stuff.
One who can see without seeming to see,
That's an observer as good as three.
With pen and with pencil we're learning to say
Nothing, more cleverly every day.

Aeolian Harp

O pale green sea,
With long, pale, purple clouds above -
What lies in me like weight of love?

What dies in me with utter grief,
Because there comes no sign
Through the sun-raying West,
Or the dim sea-line?

O salted air,
Blown round the rocky headland still,
What calls me there from cove and hill?
What calls me fair
From thee, the first-born of the youthful night,
Or in the waves is coming
Through the dusk twilight ?

O yellow Star,
Quivering upon the rippling tide -
Sendest so far to one that sigh'd?
Bendest thou, Star,
Above, where the shadows of the dead have rest
And constant silence,
With a message from the blest?

After Sunset

The vast and solemn company of clouds
Around the Sun's death, lit, incarnadined,
Cool into ashy wan; as Night enshrouds
The level pasture, creeping up behind
Through voiceless vales, o'er lawn and purpled hill
And hazéd mead, her mystery to fulfil.
Cows low from far-off farms; the loitering wind

Sighs in the hedge, you hear it if you will,--
Tho' all the wood, alive atop with wings
Lifting and sinking through the leafy nooks,
Seethes with the clamour of a thousand rooks.
Now every sound at length is hush'd away.
These few are sacred moments. One more Day
Drops in the shadowy gulf of bygone things.

Among the Heather

One evening walking out,
I o'ertook a modest colleen,
When the wind was blowing cool,
And the harvest leaves were falling.

'Is our road, by chance, the same?
Might we travel on together ?'
'O, I keep the mountain side' (she replied),
'among the heather.'

'Your mountain air is sweet
When the days are long and sunny,
When the grass grows round the rocks,
And the whin-bloom[1] smells like honey;

But the winter's coming fast,
With its foggy, snowy weather,
And you'll find it bleak and chill
On your hill, among the heather.'

William Allingham

'Whin,' furze. She praised her mountain home:
And I'll praise it too, with reason,
For where Molly is, there's sunshine
And flow'rs at every season.

Be the moorland black or white,
Does it signify a feather,
Now I know the way by heart,
Every part, among the heather?

The sun goes down in haste,
And the night falls thick and stormy;
Yet I'd travel twenty miles
To the welcome that's before me;

Singing hi for Eskydun,
In the teeth of wind and weather!
Love'll warm me as I go
Through the snow, among the heather.

Amy Margaret's Five Year Old

Amy Margaret's five years old,
Amy Margaret's hair is gold,
Dearer twenty-thousand-fold
Than gold, is Amy Margaret.
"Amy" is friend, is "Margaret"

[1]Furze or Gorse - evergreen shrub with yellow flowers.

The pearl for crown or carkanet?
Or peeping daisy, summer's pet?
Which are you, Amy Margaret?
A friend, a daisy, and a pearl,
A kindly, simple, precious girl, --
Such, howsoe'er the world may twirl,
Be ever, -- Amy Margaret!

An Evening

A sunset's mounded cloud;
A diamond evening-star;
Sad blue hills afar;
Love in his shroud.

Scarcely a tear to shed;
Hardly a word to say;
The end of a summer day;
Sweet Love dead.

Autumnal Sonnet

Now Autumn's fire burns slowly along the woods,
And day by day the dead leaves fall and melt,
And night by night the monitory blast
Wails in the key-hold, telling how it pass'd
O'er empty fields, or upland solitudes,
Or grim wide wave; and now the power is felt
Of melancholy, tenderer in its moods

Than any joy indulgent summer dealt.
Dear friends, together in the glimmering eve,
Pensive and glad, with tones that recognise
The soft invisible dew in each one's eyes,
It may be, somewhat thus we shall have leave
To walk with memory,--when distant lies
Poor Earth,
Where we were wont to live and grieve.

Bona Dea

Waking after dawn of day,
Warm and full of smiles I lay,
Safe, come good or evil hap,
In a queenly mother's lap.

Her waving skirts of flowing wind
Rustled the grass and swept behind
On hanging boughs of pathside trees,
But shook no bud nor leaf from these;

Her misty robe was rich and fair,
As a mountain's clad in soft blue air;
Her breath was like the green smells of Spring
Blowing round birds to make them sing;

Her tresses' tinge faint cloudlets hold
Where sets the sun in a flame of gold,
The while her pure face stood serene
And glowing, as the sky between;

Brooks and flow'rs her feet to grace,
All the shoreless Sea of Space
Round her and above her spread,
Doming her imperial head,
Landscapes on her garment's hem
The jewell'd night for diadem.

Ever she sung a wondrous song,
Many-toned and full and strong,
Yet drawn to whisper in my ear
As though for mine alone to hear.

The dash of floods and the chime of rills
Were in it; far on misty hills
I heard the footsteps of the thunder,
And bleating sheep in pastures under.

The lark in airy glitterings
Sparkling song from his quivering wings,
The jolly thrush-notes gay and bold,
The blackbird's vesper in thicket-fold,

The rail craik-craiking through starry shadows
Over dim lawn and darkling meadows,
The carolling redbreast from roadside spray
Or garden-wall, on an Autumn day,

And the waving, rustling sea of wheat,
Foamed at its marge with meadow-sweet,
And the whispering harebell on the leas,
And the forest-harp of the playing breeze

William Allingham

With strings of subtly varied tone,
Came in that music, every one :
And the roar and burst of the ocean waves,
And the water-chimes in heavy caves,

And the outcast wind condemn'd to grieve
Through casement-chinks on a winter eve,
And a strange-familiar melody
Of cradle-rock and lullaby,

And purring flame on a shadowy hearth,
And hum of frost to the dreaming Earth.

I was lapt in full content
When her mouth my mother bent
Down to my cheek,—and soon I knew
Where the primrose treasures grew;

And roll'd in richer garden-mines,
Tasting scents like fairy wines;
Centred in the heavens that lie
Round Childhood's short eternity.

Were they moments, were they years,
Measured out the sliding spheres—
The growing, changing, longing, dreaming,
In Me, the centre of all the seeming,

Till the hour, the hour of hours,
When she called me from my flow'rs,

When she kiss'd me on the lips,
And reveal'd from long eclipse

Fateful eyes of infinite blue
Where the living soul shone through
Like watching stars that lie soft and bright
In the violet depths of the midsummer night,

And ever still in measure sung,
While a softer spirit-tongue,
Thrilling, mystical, remote,
Echo'd every falling note,

With a ringing crystalline,
A monotony divine ?

Then a strong and joyous madness,
Then a dark and heavy sadness,
Swept across my struggling brain ;—
Deep the rapture, fierce the pain,

Ere I found myself again !
And the weak departing fever
Took away from me for ever
Much that memory can deplore,

Much, besides, that grieves me more,
Because my mind in vain is tost

To recollect what I have lost.
But now, to keep me from despair,

William Allingham

Gifts she brought, of mirrors rare,
Reflecting sea and earth and air ;
Mingling with these in magic scope
Phantoms of Memory and of Hope;

Catching her ample robe of blue,
And lighting the sapphire through and through
With inner blazes that came and went
Like angels flushing the firmament;

Showing a blossom at her feet
Orbed into a sphere complete,
Full of beauty and life and power—
The careless birth of a sunny hour;

Painting one face in colour'd flame,
With the universe for frame.
Spiritual-strange did forms appear,
And the stars and the depths of heaven drew near,

And blended mystic lights and songs
With glance and voice of earthly throngs.
What was that which lurk'd behind
To draw a fresh cloud on my mind?

For I was tempted to despise
And look upon all with unholy eyes.
My mother's pure look and royal clothing
Fill'd me with weariness and loathing;

In gentle words I began to hear
Pining, and discontent, and fear;

In louder tones a continual uttering
Of hate, and rage, and rebellious muttering;
I saw an omnipotent darkness lurk
To swallow all light, all life, all work;

All growing, changing, feeling, dreaming;
And Me, the centre of all the seeming,
Lying encrusted with painful fate,
A leper at the palace-gate.

But again she stoop'd,—I feel it now,
That heavenly kiss on my scalded brow.
There were awful thunders rolling round me ;
Harshest tearings of bands that bound me;

Stretchings of crampt, retorted limbs ;
Agony of life, as when it brims
On the wrung-out brain of a rescued man,—
And I was saved from the crushing ban.

Now I am master in my house;
Granted power to bind and loose ;
In noble heirdom set at one
With princely earth and kingly sun.

And ever doth my mother keep
Steady watch the while I sleep;

In hours of sickness still she tends me,
In hours of danger still befriends me;

And with voice that rises clearly,
Sings the hymn I love so dearly,
Hymn that seems unfolding slowly
To a sense profound and holy,

Etherizing loss and gain,
And forgetting its own strain.
She hath kiss'd my cheek, my lips, my brow.
One other kiss awaits me now,

One which I shall scarcely feel,
To close mine eyes with loving seal.
Bona Dea! live or die,
Take me, keep me, thy son am I.

The Boy

The Boy from his bedroom-window
Look'd over the little town,
And away to the bleak black upland
Under a clouded moon.

The moon came forth from her cavern,
He saw the sudden gleam
Of a tarn in the swarthy moorland;
Or perhaps the whole was a dream.

For I never could find that water
In all my walks and rides:
Far-off, in the Land of Memory,
That midnight pool abides.

Many fine things had I glimpse of,
And said, "I shall find them one day."
Whether within or without me
They were, I cannot say.

Bramble-Hill

Not much to find, not much to see,
But the air is fresh, the path is free,
On a lonely Hill where bramble grows
In tangling clumps, and the brooklet flows
Around its feet with whispering,
Leaf-tufted are the twines in Spring;

The goldfinch builds, the hare has her form;
And when the nightless days are warm,
When grass grows high and small flowers peep,
Far and wide the trailers sweep
Their pinky silver blossoms, which
Are braided with a delicate stitch.

The berries swell with Autumn's power;
Some are red and green and sour,
Some are black and juicy to bite,
Some have a maggot, some a blight.

William Allingham

Then frost-nipt leaves hang rusty and tatter'd,
With sleet and hail the bushes are batter'd,

A thorny brake on the barren hill,
Where the whistling blast blows chill.
But under the snow, amid the dark,
Sleeping waits the vernal spark.

I had neither garden nor park.
On Bramble-Hill, by brake and stone,
Many a season I wandered lone,
With laughter, and pray'r, and singing, and moan;

In gray mist and in golden light,
Under the dawn, and the starry night.
Not much to find, not much to see;
But the air was fresh, the path was free.

The Children of the Land
Are given into thy hand,
O wish'd-for future King:
Gently, boldly, take them;
All they are fit for, make them;
Teach them to work, pray, sing.

By the Morning Sea

The wind shakes up the sleepy clouds
To kiss the ruddied Morn,

And from their awful misty shrouds
The Mountains are new-born:

The Sea lies fresh with open eyes;
Night-fears and moaning dreams
Brooding like clouds on nether skies,
Have sunk below, and beams

Dance on the floor like golden flies,
Or strike with joyful gleams
Some white-wing'd ship, a wandering star
Of Ocean, piloting afar.

In brakes, in woods, in cottage eaves,
The early birds are rife,
Quick voices thrill the sprinkled leaves
In ecstasy of life;

With silent gratitude of flow'rs
The morning's breath is sweet,
And cool with dew, that freshly show'rs
Round wild things' hasty feet;

But heavenly guests of tranquil hours
To inner skies retreat,
From human thoughts of lower birth
That stir upon the waking earth.

Across a thousand leagues of land
The mighty Sun looks free,

And in their fringe of rock and sand
A thousand leagues of sea.

Lo ! I, in this majestic room,
Real as the mighty Sun,
Inherit this day and its doom
Eternally begun.

A world of men the rays illume,
God's men, and I am one.
But life that is not pure and bold
Doth tarnish every morning's gold.

Down on the Shore

Down on the shore, on the sunny shore!
Where the salt smell cheers the land;
Where the tide moves bright
Under boundless light,
And the surge on the glittering strand;
Where the children wade in the shallow pools,
Or run from the froth in play;
Where the swift little boats with milk-white wings
Are crossing the sapphire bay,
And the ship in full sail, with a fortunate gale,
Holds proudly on her way;
Where the nets are spread on the grass to dry,
And asleep, hard by, the fishermen lie,
Under the tent of the warm blue sky,

With the hushing wave on its golden floor
To sing their lullaby.

Down on the shore, on the stormy shore!
Beset by a growling sea,
Whose mad waves leap on the rocky steep
Like wolves up a traveller's tree;
Where the foam flies wide, and an angry blast
Blows the curlew off, with a screech;
Where the brown sea-wrack, torn up by the roots,
Is flung out of fishes' reach;
And the tall ship rolls on the hidden shoals,
And scatters her planks on the beach;
Where slate and straw through the village spin,
And a cottage fronts the fiercest din
With a sailor's wife sitting sad within,
Hearkening the wind and the water's roar,
Till at last her tears begin.

The Eviction

In early morning twilight, raw and chill,
Damp vapours brooding on the barren hill,
Through miles of mire in steady grave array
Threescore well-arm'd police pursue their way;
Each tall and bearded man a rifle swings,
And under each greatcoat a bayonet clings:
The Sheriff on his sturdy cob astride
Talks with the chief, who marches by their side,
And, creeping on behind them, Paudeen Dhu

Pretends his needful duty much to rue.
Six big-boned labourers, clad in common freize,
Walk in the midst, the Sheriff's staunch allies;
Six crowbar men, from distant county brought, -
Orange, and glorying in their work, 'tis thought,
But wrongly,- churls of Catholics are they,
And merely hired at half a crown a day.

The hamlet clustering on its hill is seen,
A score of petty homesteads, dark and mean;
Poor always, not despairing until now;
Long used, as well as poverty knows how,
With life's oppressive trifles to contend.
This day will bring its history to an end.
Moveless and grim against the cottage walls
Lean a few silent men: but someone calls
Far off; and then a child 'without a stitch'
Runs out of doors,
Flies back with piercing screech,
And soon from house to house is heard the cry
Of female sorrow, swelling loud and high,
Which makes the men
Blaspheme between their teeth.
Meanwhile, o'er fence and watery field beneath,

The little army moves through drizzling rain;
A 'Crowbar' leads the Sheriff's nag;
The lane is enter'd,
And their plashing tramp draws near,
One instant, outcry holds its breath to hear

"Halt!" - at the doors they form in double line,
And ranks of polish'd rifles wetly shine.
The Sheriff's painful duty must be done;
He begs for quiet-and the work's begun.
The strong stand ready; now appear the rest,
Girl, matron, grandsire, baby on the breast,
And Rosy's thin face on a pallet borne;
A motley concourse, feeble and forlorn.
One old man, tears upon his wrinkled cheek,
Stands trembling on a threshold, tries to speak,
But, in defect of any word for this,
Mutely upon the doorpost prints a kiss,
Then passes out for ever. Through the crowd
The children run bewilder'd, wailing loud;
Where needed most, the men combine their aid;
And, last of all, is Oona forth convey'd,

Reclined in her accustom'd strawen chair,
Her aged eyelids closed, her thick white hair
Escaping from her cap; she feels the chill,
Looks round and murmurs, then again is still.
Now bring the remnants of each household fire;
On the wet ground the hissing coals expire;
And Paudeen Dhu, with meekly dismal face,
Receives the full possession of the place.

William Allingham

The Fairies

Up the airy mountain,
Down the rushy glen,
We daren't go a-hunting
For fear of little men;
Wee folk, good folk,
Trooping all together;
Green jacket, red cap,
And white owl's feather!

Down along the rocky shore
Some make their home,
They live on crispy pancakes
Of yellow tide-foam;
Some in the reeds
Of the black mountain lake,
With frogs for their watch-dogs,
All night awake.

High on the hill-top
The old King sits;
He is now so old and gray
He's nigh lost his wits.
With a bridge of white mist
Columbkill he crosses,
On his stately journeys
From Slieveleague to Rosses;
Or going up with music

On cold starry nights
To sup with the Queen
Of the gay Northern Lights.

They stole little Bridget
For seven years long;
When she came down again
Her friends were all gone.
They took her lightly back,
Between the night and morrow,
They thought that she was fast asleep,
But she was dead with sorrow.
They have kept her ever since
Deep within the lake,
On a bed of flag-leaves,
Watching till she wake.

By the craggy hill-side,
Through the mosses bare,
They have planted thorn-trees
For pleasure here and there.
If any man so daring
As dig them up in spite,
He shall find their sharpest thorns
In his bed at night.

Up the airy mountain,
Down the rushy glen,
We daren't go a-hunting
For fear of little men;
Wee folk, good folk,

Trooping all together;
Green jacket, red cap,
And white owl's feather!

Footsteps

Sound of feet, In the lonely street,
Coming to-night,—coming to me?
Perhaps (why not? it well may be)

My dear old friend
From the world's end,
At last.
How we shall meet,
And shout and greet,

(O hearty voice that memory knows !)
Till the first gush and rush be past,
And smoother now the current flows;
Plenty on either side to tell, Sharing joy,
And soothing pain
As friendship's tongue can do so well.

Hush! hark!
I hear, in the dark—
Only the footsteps of the rain.

Stay! stay!
Coming this way
Through the dull night—

Perhaps to me—
Coming, coming, coming fast,
(And why may not such things be?)

A messenger's feet
In the lonely street,
With some good wonderful news to say
At last.

A word has been spoken,
A bad spell broken,
Men see aright,
All faces are bright,
For the world to-morrow begins anew;
There's much to plan, and plenty to do ;
Away ! search, sift the country through,
And say at once to a certain few:

'Come, for our gain, We know you,
And now we have work for you
Hush! hark!
I hear, in the dark—
Only the footsteps of the rain.

Close, close,
Outside the house, Steps approaching!—
Are these for me?
Coming gently, coming fast,

(And O, if this can be !)—
Out of the strife

Of selfish life
My Love has fled of a sudden,—'tis She,
At last!

Here she stands,
Eyes and mouth and tender form
True and warm;
My dream of many a lonely year;
Stretches her hands—
No doubt or fear—
' See, my Love, 'tis all in vain
To keep true lovers parted,
If they be faithful-hearted !'

Hush ! hark !
I hear, in the dark—
Only the footsteps of the rain.

Half-Waking

I thought it was the little bed
I slept in long ago;
A straight white curtain at the head,
And two smooth knobs below.
I thought I saw the nursery fire,
And in a chair well-known
My mother sat, and did not tire
With reading all alone.
If I should make the slightest sound
To show that I'm awake,

She'd rise, and lap the blankets round,
My pillow softly shake;
Kiss me, and turn my face to see
The shadows on the wall,
And then sing Rousseau's Dream to me,
Till fast asleep I fall.
But this is not my little bed;
That time is far away;
With strangers now I live instead,
From dreary day to day.

In a Garden

Betwixt our apple-boughs, how clear
The violet western hills appear,
As calmly ends another day
Of Earth's long history,—from the ray
She with slow majestic motion
Wheeling continent and ocean
Into her own dim shade, wherethrough
The Outer Heavens come into view,

Deep beyond deep.
In thought conceive
This rolling Globe whereon we live
(For in the mind, and there alone
A picture of the world is shown),

How huge it is, how full of things,
As round the royal Sun it swings,

William Allingham

In one of many subject rings—
Carrying our Cottage with the rest,
Its rose-lawn and its martin's nest.

But, number every grain of sand
Wherever salt wave touches land;
Number in single drops the sea;
Number the leaves on every tree;

Number Earth's living creatures, all
That run, that fly, that swim, that crawl;
Of sands, drops, leaves, and lives, the count
Add up into one vast amount;

And then, for every separate one
Of all those, let a flaming Sun
Whirl in the boundless skies,
With each Its massy planets,
To outreach All sight, all thought:
For all we see, Encircled with Infinity,
Is but an island.

Look aloft,
The stars are gathering.
Cool and soft
The twilight in our garden-croft
Purples the crimson-folded rose,
(O tell me how so sweet it grows)
Makes gleam like stars the cluster'd white;
And Beauty too is infinite.

In Highgate Cemetary

Far-spread below doth London wear
Its cloud by day, its fire by night;
But scarce with heavenly presence there,
Enshrined in smoke or pallid light.

Incessant troops from that vast throng
Withdraw to silent colonies ;
Where houses, lo, are fair and strong,
Though ruins all that dwell in these.

Yet here, too, under boundless sky,
Do children sport, and wild birds sing;
Calm foliage waxes green and high,
And grave-side roses smell of Spring.

In a Spring Grove

Here the white-ray'd anemone is born,
Wood-sorrel, and the varnish'd buttercup;
And primrose in its purfled green swathed up,
Pallid and sweet round every budding thorn,
Gray ash, and beech with rusty leaves outworn.
Here, too the darting linnet hath her nest
In the blue-lustred holly, never shorn,
Whose partner cheers her little brooding breast,
Piping from some near bough. O simple song!

O cistern deep of that harmonious rillet,
And these fair juicy stems that climb and throng
The vernal world, and unexhausted seas
Of flowing life, and soul that asks to fill it,
Each and all of these,--
And more, and more than these!

In Snow

O English mother, in the ruddy glow
Hugging your baby closer when outside
You see the silent, soft, and cruel snow
Falling again, and think what ills betide
Unshelter'd creatures,--your sad thoughts may go
Where War and Winter now, two spectre-wolves,
Hunt in the freezing vapour that involves
Those Asian peaks of ice and gulfs below.
Does this young Soldier heed the snow that fills
His mouth and open eyes? or mind, in truth,
To-night, his mother's parting syllables?
Ha! is't a red coat?--Merely blood. Keep ruth
For others; this is but an Afghan youth
Shot by the stranger on his native hills.

Invitation to a Painter

Flee from London, good my Walter!
Boundless jail of bricks and gas;
Care not if your Exhibition

Swarm with portrait and Gil Bias,
Or with marvels dear to Ruskin;
Fly the swelter, fly the crush,
British Mammon in his glory,—
In his breathless race and rush.

Leave the hot tumultuous city
For the breakers' rival roar,
Quit your soft suburban landscape
For the rude hills by the shore,

Leagues of smoke for morning vapour
Lifted off a mountain-range,
Crinoline for barefoot beauty,
And for " something new and strange"
All your towny wit and gossip.
You shall both in field and fair,
Paddy's cunning and politeness
With the Cockney ways compare,
Catch those lilts and old-world tunes
The maidens at their needle sing,
Peep at dancers, from an outskirt
Of the blithe applausive ring,

See our petty Court of Justice,
Where the swearing's very strong,
See our little plain St. Peter's
With its kneeling peasant throng;
Hear the brogue and Gaelic round you;
Sketch a hundred Irish scenes,
(Not mere whisky and shillelagh)—

William Allingham

Wedding banquets, funeral keenes;
Rove at pleasure, noon or midnight;
Change a word with all you meet;
Ten times safer than in England,
Far less trammell'd in your feet.

Here, the only danger known
Is walking where the land's your own.
Landscape-lords are left alone.

We are barren, I confess it;
But our scope of view is fine;
Dignifying shapes of mountains
Wave on each horizon-line,
So withdrawn that never house-room
Utmost pomp of cloud may lack,
Dawn or sunset, moon or planet,
Or mysterious zodiac.
Hills beneath run all a-wrinkle,
Rocky, moory, pleasant green;
From its Lough the Flood descending,
Flashes like a sword between,

Through our crags and woods and meadows,
To the mounded harbour-sand,
To the Bay, calm blue, or, sometimes,
Whose Titanic arms expand;
Welcome to the mighty billow
Rolling in from Newfoundland.
Oats, potatoes, cling in patches
Round the rocks and boulder-stones,

Like a motley ragged garment
For the lean Earth's jutting bones;
Moors extend, and bogs and furzes,
Where you seldom meet a soul,

But the Besom-man or woman,
Who to earn a stingy dole;
Stoops beneath a nodding burden
Of the scented heather-plant,
Or a jolly gaiter'd Sportsman,
Striding near the grouse's haunt,—

Slow the anchoritic heron,
Musing by his voiceless pond,
Startled, with the startled echo
On the lonely cliff beyond,
Rising, flaps away.
And now a summit shows us,
Wide and bare,
All the brown uneven country,
Lit with waters here and there;
Southward, mountains—northward, mountains—
Westward, golden mystery
Of coruscation, when the Daystar
Flings his largesse on the sea;

Peasant cots with humble haggarts;
Mansions with obsequious groves;
A Spire, a Steeple, rival standards,
Which the liberal distance loves
To set in union.

William Allingham

There the dear but dirty little Town abides,
And you and I come home to dinner
After all our walks and rides;

You shall taste a cleanly pudding;
But, bring shoes to stand a mudding.

Let me take you by the murvagh[1],
Sprinkled with the Golden Weeds[2],
Merry troops of Irish Fairies
Mount by moonlight for their steeds,—
Wherefore sacred and abundant
Over all the land are they.
Many cows are feeding through it;
Cooling, of a sultry day,

By the River's brink, that journeys
Under Fairy Hill, and past,
Gentle cadences of landscape
Sloping to the sea at last.
Now the yellow sand is round us,
Drifted in fantastic shapes,
Heights and hollows, forts and bastions,
Pyramids and curving capes,
Breezy ridges thinly waving
With the bent-weed's pallid green,

[1] "Murvagh," level place near the sea, salt marsh.
[2] "Golden Weeds," ragwort, called "boughaleen
bwee" (little yellow boy), also "fairy-horse."

Delicate for eye that sips it,
Till a better feast is seen

Where the turf swells thick-embroider'd
With the fragrant purple thyme,
Where, in plots of speckled orchis,
Poet larks begin their rhyme,
Honey'd galium wafts an invitation
To the gypsy bees,
Rabbits' doorways wear for garlands
Azure tufts of wild heartsease,
Paths of sward around the hillocks,
Dipping into ferny dells,
Show you heaps of childhood's treasure—
Twisted, vary-tinted shells.

Lapt in moss and blossoms, empty,
And forgetful of the wave.
Ha! a creature scouring nimbly,
Hops at once into his cave;
Brother Coney sits regardant,—
Wink an eye, and where is he ?
Towns and villages we pass through,
But the people skip and flee. . .
Over sandy slope, a Mountain
Lifts afar his fine blue head;
There the savage twins of eagles,
Gaping, hissing to be fed,

Welcome back their wide-wing'd parent
With a rabbit scarcely dead

Hung in those powerful yellow claws,
And gorge the bloody flesh and fur
On ledge of rock, their cradle.
Shepherd-boy! with limbs and voice bestir
To your watch of tender lambkins
On a lonesome valley-side,
If you, careless in the sunshine,
See a rapid shadow glide ;
Down the verdant undercliff.
Afar that conquering eye can sweep

Mountain-glens, and may, and warren,
To the margin of the deep,
Worse than dog or ferret,—vanish
From your gold-green-mossy dells,
Nibbling natives of the burrow !
Seek your inmost winding cells
When such cruelties appear;
But a Painter do not fear,
Nor a Poet, loitering near.

Painter, what is spread before you?
'Tis the great Atlantic sea!
Many-colour'd floor of ocean,
Where the lights and shadows flee;
Waves and wavelets running landward
With a sparkle and a song,
Crystal green with foam enwoven,
Bursting, brightly spilt along;
Thousand living shapes of wonder
In the clear pools of the rock;

Lengths of strand, and seafowl armies
Rising like a puff of smoke;

Drift and tangle on the limit
Where the wandering water fails;
Level faintly-clear horizon,
Touch'd with clouds and Phantom sails,—
O come hither! weeks together
Let us watch the big Atlantic,
Blue or purple, green or gurly,
Dark or shining, smooth or frantic.

Far across the tide, slow-heaving,
Rich autumnal daylight sets;
See our crowd of busy row-boats,
Hear us noisy with our nets,
Where the glittering sprats in millions
From the rising mesh are stript,
Till there scarce is room for rowing,
Every gunwale nearly dipt;
Gulls around us, flying, dropping,
Thick in air as flakes of snow,
Snatching luckless little fishes
In their silvery overflow.

Now one streak of western scarlet
Lingers upon ocean's edge,
Now through ripples of the splendour
Of the moon we swiftly wedge
Our loaded bows; the fisher-hamlet
Beacons with domestic light;

William Allingham

On the shore the carts and horses
Wait to travel through the night
To a distant city market,
While the boatmen sup and sleep,
While the firmamental stillness
Arches o'er the dusky deep,

Ever muttering chaunts and dirges
Round its rocks and sandy verges.
Ere we part at winter's portal,
I shall row you of a night
On a swirling Stygian river,
To a ghostly yellow light.
When the nights are black and gusty,
Then do eels in myriads glide
Through the pools and down the rapids,
Hurrying to the ocean-tide,—
But they fear the frost or moonshine,
In their mud-beds coiling close—
And the wearmen, on the platform
Of that pigmy water-house

Built among the river-currents,
With a dam to either bank,
Pull the purse-net's heavy end
To swing across their wooden tank,
Ere they loose the cord about it—
Then a slimy wriggling heap
Falls with splashing, where a thousand
Fellowprisoners heave and creep.

Chill winds roar above the wearmen,
Darkling rush the floods below;

There they watch and work their eel-nets,
Till the late dawn lets them go.

There we'll join their eely supper,
Bearing smoke the best we can,
(House's furniture a salt-box,
Truss of straw, and frying-pan),
Hearken Con's astounding stories,
How a mytho logic eel
Chased a man o'er miles of country,
Swallow'd two dogs at a meal,
To the hissing bubbling music
Of the pan and pratie-pot.
Denser grows the reek around us,
Each like Mussulman a-squat,

Each with victuals in his fingers,
We devour them hot and hot;
Smoky rays our lantern throwing,
Ruddy peat-fire warmly glowing,
Noisily the River flowing.

But first of all—the time's at hand
To journey to our Holy Well,
Clear as when the old Saint bless'd it,
Rising in its rock-bound cell.
Two great Crosses, carved in bosses,
Curves, and fillets interlacing,

William Allingham

Spread their aged arms of stone,
As if in sempiternal blessing;
Five much-wrinkled thorntrees bend,
As though in everlasting pray'r.
Greenly shines the growing crop,
Along the shelter'd hill-side there;

But the tristful little Abbey,
Crumbling among weeds and grass,
Nevermore can suns or seasons
Bring a smile to as they pass;
By a window-gap or mullion
Creeps the fringe of ivy leaves,
Nettles crowd the sculptured doorway,
Where the wind goes through and grieves;
Sad the tender blue of harebells
On its ledges low and high;
Merry singing of the goldfinch
There sounds pensive as a sigh.

'Tis a day of summer: see you,
How the pilgrims wend along;
Scarlet petticoat, blue mantle,
Grey frieze, mingling in the throng.
By the pathway sit the Beggars,
Each an ailment and a whine;
Lame and sickly figures pass them,
Tottering in that pilgrim line;
Children carried by their parents,
Very loth to let them die;

Lovely girls too, with their eyelids
Downcast on a rosary;

Shrunken men, and witch-like women;
Young men in their proudest prime;
Guilty foreheads, hot-blood faces,
Penance-vow'd for secret crime.
All by turn, in slow procession,
Pace the venerable bounds,
Barefoot, barehead, seven times duly
Kneeling in tĽ accustom'd rounds;
Thrice among the hoary ruins,
Once before the wasted shrine,
Once at each great carven cross,
And once to form the Mystic Sign,

Dipping reverential finger
In the Well, on brow and breast.
Meanwhile worn and wan, the Sick
Under those rooted thorntrees rest,
Waiting sadly. Here are human
Figures of our land and day,
On a thousand-years-old background,—
Still in keeping, it and they!
Walter, make a vow nor break it;
Turn your pilgrim steps our way.
O might you come, before there fell
One hawthorn-flow'r in Columb's Well!

William Allingham

John Clodd

John Clodd was greatly troubled in his mind,
But reason for the same could noways find.
Says he, 'I'll go to Mary; I've no doubt,
If any mortal can, she'll vind it out.'
'Why, John, what is the matter? where dost ail?
In 'ead or stummick! eh, thou dost look pale.
Can't ait? can't sleep? yet nayther sick nor sore?
Ne'er felt the like in all thy life afore?

Why, lad, I'll tell 'ee what,—thou beest in love.'
John look'd at Mary, gave his hat a shove,
And rubb'd his chin awhile, and mutter'd 'There!
Only to think o' that!'—then from a stare
Broke by degrees into a smile, half-witted,
'Dang! Mary, I don't know but what you've hit it!

I thought on no sich thing, but now I see
Tis plain as haystack. Yaas, in love I be !
But who be I in love wi', Mary ? Come !'
'Why, can't yo' tell that, John? Art blind, or dumb?

Is't Emma White? or Liz? or Dora Peak?
Or pirty little Sue? or Widow Sleek?
Or Tilda Rudlip, now? or Martha's Jane?
Or Squire's new Dairymaid? or old Miss Elaine,
Wi' lots o' money? Don't be angry, John,

I've guess'd all round,—you hates 'em every one?
Still, you loves zumbody. . . . Mayhap 'tis me?'

'Why, Mary, what a clever lass you be!
I never once took thought on such a thing;
But you it is, and no one else, by Jing!'
'Well, John, that's settled; so Good-night at last.'
'No, Mary, don'tee run away so fast!
What next are we to do?'
'What next? O bother! Get married, I suppose,
sometime or other.'
'Right, lass, again! I niver thought o' that.
How do'ee iver vind out things so pat?
But stop a minute, Mary,—
Tell me how Does folk— . . .
She's off! I'm fairly puzzled now!'

'Why, yes—we've pass'd a pleasant day;
While life's true joys are on their way,'
Ah, me! I now look back afar,
And see that one day like a star.
Everything passes and vanishes;
Everything leaves its trace ;
And often you see in a footstep
What you could not see in a face.

William Allingham

Kitty O'Hea

Now, Kitty O'Hea, darling jewel,
I wish you'd consider my case !
O, who could believe you're so cruel
To look in that beautiful face ?
Let roses be jealous,—no matter!
The sunshine's in love with your cheek;
What singing-bird wouldn't I flatter
To say it's her voice when you speak ?
Kitty O'Hea, O'Hea,
Kitty, give ear to my song.
Kitty O'Hea, O'Hea,
Kitty, I'm courting you long.

My thoughts I can never keep steady,
No more nor a man in a dream,
They caper like straws in an eddy,
In place of pursuing the stream.
Amusement or meat I don't care for,
I moan like a cow gone astray;
Myself knows the why and the wherefore,-
I'm thinking of Kitty O'Hea.
Kitty O'Hea, O'Hea, etc.

I never objected, in reason,
To bear with a slight or a scoff,
But snow isn't always in season,
And Lent isn't very far off.

Shrove-Tuesday's the time for to shake one,
And single I'll not pass the day,
Young, old, maid or widow, I'll take one,—
So mind yourself, Kitty O'Hea !
Kitty O'Hea, O'Hea,
Kitty, give heed to my song.
Kitty O'Hea, O'Hea,
Kitty, I'm courting too long !

Late Autumn

October - and the skies are cool and gray
O'er stubbles emptied of their latest sheaf,
Bare meadow, and the slowly falling leaf.
The dignity of woods in rich decay
Accords full well with this majestic grief
That clothes our solemn purple hills to-day,
Whose afternoon is hush'd, and wintry brief
Only a robin sings from any spray.

And night sends up her pale cold moon, and spills
White mist around the hollows of the hills,
Phantoms of firth or lake; the peasant sees
His cot and stockyard, with the homestead trees,
Islanded; but no foolish terror thrills
His perfect harvesting; he sleeps at ease.

William Allingham

The Lepracaun or Fairy Shoemaker

Little Cowboy, what have you heard,
Up on the lonely rath's green mound?
Only the plaintive yellow bird
Sighing in sultry fields around,
Chary, chary, chary, chee-ee! -
Only the grasshopper and the bee? -
"Tip-tap, rip-rap,
Tick-a-tack-too!

Scarlet leather, sewn together,
This will make a shoe.
Left, right, pull it tight;
Summer days are warm;
Underground in winter,
Laughing at the storm!"
Lay your ear close to the hill.

Do you not catch the tiny clamour,
Busy click of an elfin hammer.
Voice of the Lepracaun singing shrill
As he merrily plies his trade?
He's a span
And a quarter in height,
Get him in sight, hold him tight,
And you're a made Man!

You watch your cattle the summerday,
Sup on potatoes, sleep in the hay;
How would you like to roll in your carriage,
Look for a duchess's daughter in marriage?
Seize the shoemaker - then you may!
"Big boots a -hunting,
Sandals in the hall,
White for a wedding feast,
Pink for a ball.

This way, that way,
So we make a shoe;
Getting rich every stitch,
Tick-a-tack too!"
Nine and ninety treasure crocks
This keen miser fairy hath,
Hid in the mountains, woods and rocks,
Ruin and round-tow'r, cave and rath,
And where cormorants build;
From times of old
Guarded by him;
Each of them fill'd
Full to the brim
With gold!
I caught him at work one day, myself,
In the castle ditch where fox-glove grows, -
A wrinkled, wizen'd and bearded Elf,
Spectacles stuck on his pointed nose,
Silver buckles to his hose,
Leather apron - shoe in his lap -
'Rip-rap, tip-tap,

Tick-tack-too!
(A grasshopper on my cap!
Away the moth flew!)

Buskins for a fairy prince,
Brogues for his son -
Pay me well, pay me well,
When the job is done!"
The rogue was mine, beyond a doubt.
I stared at him, he stared at me;
"Servant Sir!" "Humph" says he,
And pull'd a snuff-box out.

He took a long pinch, look'd better pleased,
The queer little Lepracaun;
Offer'd the box with a whimsical grace, -
Pouf! He flung the dust in my face,
And while I sneezed,
Was gone!

The Little Dell

Doleful was the land,
Dull on, every side,
Neither soft nor grand,
Barren, bleak, and wide;
Nothing look'd with love;
All was dingy brown;
The very skies above
Seem'd to sulk and frown.

Plodding sick and sad,
Weary day on day;
Searching, never glad,
Many a miry way;
Poor existence lagg'd
In this barren place;
While the seasons dragg'd
Slowly o'er its face.

Spring, to sky and ground,
Came before I guess'd;
Then one day I found
A valley, like a nest!
Guarded with a spell
Sure it must have been,
This little fairy dell
Which I had never seen.

Open to the blue,
Green banks hemm'd it round
A rillet wander'd through
With a tinkling sound;
Briars among the rocks
Tangled arbours made;
Primroses in flocks
Grew beneath their shade.

Merry birds a few,
Creatures wildly tame,
Perch'd and sung and flew;

Timid field-mice came;
Beetles in the moss
Journey'd here and there;
Butterflies across
Danced through sunlit air.

There I often read,
Sung alone, or dream'd;
Blossoms overhead,
Where the west wind stream'd;
Small horizon-line,
Smoothly lifted up,

Held this world of mine
In a grassy cup.

The barren land to-day
Hears my last adieu:
Not an hour I stay;
Earth is wide and new.
Yet, farewell, farewell!
May the sun and show'rs
Bless that Little Dell
Of safe and tranquil hours!

Lovely Mary Donnelly

Oh, lovely Mary Donnelly,
My joy, my only best!
If fifty girls were round you,

I'd hardly see the rest;
Be what it may the time o' day,
The place be where it will,
Sweet looks o' Mary Donnelly,
They bloom before me still.

Her eyes like mountain water
That's flowing on a rock,
How clear they are, how dark they are!
They give me many a shock;

Red rowans warm in sunshine
And wetted with a show'r,
Could ne'er express the charming lip
That has me in its pow'r.

Her nose is straight and handsome,
Her eyebrows lifted up,
Her chin is very neat and pert,
And smooth like a china cup,

Her hair's the brag of Ireland,
So weighty and so fine;
It's rolling down upon her neck,
And gather'd in a twine.

The dance o' last Whit-Monday night
Exceeded all before,
No pretty girl for miles about
Was missing from the floor;

William Allingham

But Mary kept the belt o' love,
And O but she was gay!
She danced a jig, she sung a song,
That took my heart away.

When she stood up for dancing,
Her steps were so complete
The music nearly kill'd itself
To listen to her feet;

The fiddler moan'd his blindness,
He heard her so much praised,
But bless'd his luck to not be deaf
When once her voice she raised.

And evermore I'm whistling
Or lilting what you sung,
Your smile is always in my heart,
Your name beside my tongue;

But you've as many sweethearts
As you'd count on both your hands,
And for myself there's not a thumb
Or little finger stands.

Tis you're the flower o' womankind
In country or in town;
The higher I exalt you,
The lower I'm cast down.

If some great lord should come this way,
And see your beauty bright,
And you to be his lady,
I'd own it was but right.

O might we live together
In a lofty palace hall,
Where joyful music rises,
And where scarlet curtains fall!

O might we live together
In a cottage mean and small,
With sods o' grass the only roof,
And mud the only wall!

O lovely Mary Donnelly,
Your beauty's my distress,
It's far too beauteous to be mine,
But I'll never wish it less.

The proudest place would fit your face,
And I am poor and low;
But blessings be about you, dear,
Wherever you may go !

Love's Insight

Who could say that Love is blind ?
Piercing-sighted, he will find

William Allingham

A thousand subtle charms that lie
Hid from every common eye.

You that love not, blind are ye,
Learn to love, and learn to see.
Tis the insight of the lover
Beauty's essence can discover.

Meadowsweet

Through grass, through amber'd cornfields,
Our slow Stream--
Fringed with its flags and reeds and rushes tall,
And Meadowsweet, the chosen of them all
By wandering children, yellow as the cream
Of those great cows--winds on as in a dream
By mill and footbridge, hamlet old and small
(Red roofs, gray tower), and sees the sunset gleam
On mullion'd windows of an ivied Hall.

There, once upon a time, the heavy King
Trod out its perfume from the Meadowsweet,
Strown like a woman's love beneath his feet,
In stately dance or jovial banqueting,
When all was new; and in its wayfaring

Our Streamlet curved, as now,
Through grass and wheat.

The Milkmaid

O Where are you going so early ? he said;
Good luck go with you, my pretty maid;
To tell you my mind I'm half afraid,
But I wish I were your sweetheart.
When the morning sun is shining low,
And the cocks in every farmyard crow,
I'll carry your pail
O'er hill and dale,
And I'll go with you a-milking.

I'm going a-milking, sir, says she,
Through the dew, and across the lea;
You ne'er would even yourself to me,
Or take me for your sweetheart.
          When the morning sun, etc.

Now give me your milking-stool awhile,
To carry it down to yonder stile ;
I'm wishing every step a mile,
And myself your only sweetheart,
          When the morning sun, etc.

Oh, here's the stile in-under the tree, And there's
the path in the grass for me,
And I thank you kindly, sir, says she,
And wish you a better sweetheart.
          When the morning sun, etc.

William Allingham

Now give me your milking-pail, says he, And
while we're going across the lea,
Pray reckon your master's cows to me,
Although I'm not your sweetheart.
      When the morning sun, etc.

Two of them red, and two of them white,
Two of them yellow and silky bright,
She told him her master's cows aright,
Though he was not her sweetheart.
      When the morning sun, etc.

She sat and milk'd in the morning sun,
And when her milking was over and done,
She found him waiting, all as one
As if he were her sweetheart.
      When the morning sun, etc.

He freely offer'd his heart and hand ;
Now she has a farm at her command,
And cows of her own to graze the land;
Success to all true sweethearts !

When the morning sun is shining low,
And the cocks in every farmyard crow,
I'll carry your pail O'er hill and dale,
And I'll go with you a-milking.

The Old Tune (Air—Colleen Dhas)

'MONGST the green Irish hills I love dearly,
At the close of a bright summer day,
I heard an old tune lilted clearly,
That sooth'd half my sorrows away.

And far o'er the wide-rolling ocean
Methinks I am hearing it now,
As a farewell of tender emotion,—
'The Pretty Girl Milking her Cow.'

Next day was the last look of Erin;
Twas almost like death to depart;
And since, in my foreign wayfaring,
That tune's like a thread round my heart

Still back to the dear old Green Island
It draws me, I cannot tell how,
The whisper in music of my land,—
'The Pretty Girl Milking her Cow.'

On a Forenoon of Spring

I'm glad I am alive, to see and feel
The full deliciousness of this bright day,
That's like a heart with nothing to conceal;
The young leaves scarcely trembling; the blue-grey

William Allingham

Rimming the cloudless ether far away;
Brairds, hedges, shadows; mountains that reveal
Soft sapphire; this great floor of polished steel
Spread out amidst the landmarks of the bay.

I stoop in sunshine to our circling net
From the black gunwale; tend these milky kine
Up their rough path; sit by yon cottage-door
Plying the diligent thread; take wings and soar--
O hark how with the season's laureate
Joy culminates in song! If such a song were mine!

Places and Men

In Sussex here, by shingle and by sand,
Flat fields and farmsteads
In their wind-blown trees,
The shallow tide-wave courses to the land,
And all along the down a fringe one sees
Of ducal woods. That 'dim discovered spire'
Is Chichester, where Collins felt a fire
Touch his sad lips;
Thatched Felpham roofs are these,
Where happy Blake found heaven
More close at hand.

Goodwood and Arundel possess their lords,
Successive in the towers and groves, which stay;
These two poor men, by some right of their own,
Possessed the earth and sea, the sun and moon,

The inner sweet of life; and put in words
A personal force that doth not pass away.

The Queen of the Forest

Beautiful, beautiful Queen of the Forest,
How art thou hidden so wondrous deep ?
Bird never sung there, fay never morriced,
All the trees are asleep.

Nigh the drizzling waterfall
Plumed ferns wave and wither ;
Voices from the woodlands call,
'Hither, O hither!'

Calling all the summer day,
Through the woodlands, far away.
Who by the rivulet loiters and lingers,
Tranced by a mirror, a murmur, a freak;
Thrown where the grass's cool fine fingers
Play with his dreamful cheek?

Cautious creatures gliding by,
Mystic sounds fill his pleasure,
Tangled roof inlaid with sky,
Flowers, heaps of treasure:

Wandering slowly all the day,
Through the woodlands, far away.

William Allingham

Late last night, betwixt moonlight and morning,
Came She, unthought of, and stood by his bed:
A kiss for love, and a kiss for warning,
A kiss for trouble and dread.

Now her flitting fading gleam
Haunts the woodlands wide and lonely;
Now, a half-remember'd dream
For his comrade only,

He shall stray the livelong day
Through the forest, far away.
Dare not the hiding Enchantress to follow!
Hearken the yew, he hath secrets of hers.
The gray owl stirs in an oaktree's hollow,

The wind in the gloomy firs.
Down among those dells of green,
Glimpses, whispers, run to wile thee;
Waking eyes have nowhere seen

Her that would beguile thee—
Draw thee on, till death of day,
Through the dusk woods, far away.

Robin Redbreast

Good-bye, good-bye to Summer!
For Summer's nearly done;
The garden smiling faintly,
Cool breezes in the sun;
Our Thrushes now are silent,
Our Swallows flown away, --
But Robin's here, in coat of brown,
With ruddy breast-knot gay.

Robin, Robin Redbreast,
O Robin dear!
Robin singing sweetly
In the falling of the year.
Bright yellow, red, and orange,
The leaves come down in hosts;
The trees are Indian Princes,
But soon they'll turn to Ghosts;

The scanty pears and apples
Hang russet on the bough,
It's Autumn, Autumn, Autumn late,
'Twill soon be Winter now.
Robin, Robin Redbreast,
O Robin dear!
And welaway! my Robin,
For pinching times are near.

William Allingham

The fireside for the Cricket,
The wheatstack for the Mouse,
When trembling night-winds whistle
And moan all round the house;
The frosty ways like iron,
The branches plumed with snow, --

Alas! in Winter, dead and dark,
Where can poor Robin go?

Robin, Robin Redbreast,
O Robin dear!
And a crumb of bread for Robin,
His little heart to cheer.

Solus

Autumn and sunset now have double-dyed
The foliage and the fern of this deep wood,
The sky above it melting placidly
All crimsonings to gray.
No sound is heard.
The Spirit of the Place, like mine, seems lull'd
In pensive retrospection.
One more Spring,
And one more Summer past,
And one more Year.

Anon the distant bell begins to chime,
And calls me homeward,

Calls me to a home
As lonely as the Forest,
Peopled but With memories,
And fantasies, and shadows.
These wait for me this evening.
What beyond? . . .
The silent sunset of a lonely life?

Song

O Spirit of the Summertime !
Bring back the roses to the dells;

The swallow from her distant clime,
The honey-bee from drowsy cells.

Bring back the friendship of the sun;
The gilded evenings, calm and late,

When merry children homeward run,
And peeping stars bid lovers wait.

Bring back the singing; and the scent
Of meadowlands at dewy prime ;—

Oh, bring again my heart's content,
Thou Spirit of the Summertime!

William Allingham

These Little Songs

These little Songs,
Found here and there,
Floating in air
By forest and lea,
Or hill-side heather,
In houses and throngs,
Or down by the sea -
Have come together,

How, I can't tell:
But I know full well
No witty goose-wing
On an inkstand begot 'em;
Remember each place
And moment of grace,
In summer or spring,
Winter or autumn

By sun, moon, stars,
Or a coal in the bars,
In market or church,
Graveyard or dance,
When they came without search,
Were found as by chance.
A word, a line,
You may say are mine;

But the best in the songs,
Whatever it be,
To you, and to me,
And to no one belongs.

The Touchstone

A man there came, whence none could tell,
Bearing a Touchstone in his hand;
And tested all things in the land
By its unerring spell.

Quick birth of transmutation smote
The fair to foul, the foul to fair;
Purple nor ermine did he spare,
Nor scorn the dusty coat.

Of heirloom jewels, prized so much,
Were many changed to chips and clods,
And even statues of the Gods
Crumbled beneath its touch.

Then angrily the people cried,
"The loss outweighs the profit far;
Our goods suffice us as they are
We will not have them tried."

William Allingham

And since they could not so prevail
To check this unrelenting guest,
They seized him, saying - "Let him test
How real it is, our jail!"

But, though they slew him with the sword,
And in a fire his Touchstone burn'd,
Its doings could not be o'erturned,
Its undoings restored.

And when to stop all future harm,
They strew'd its ashes on the breeze;
They little guess'd each grain of these
Convey'd the perfect charm.

North, south, in rings and amulets,
Throughout the crowded world 'tis borne;
Which, as a fashion long outworn,
In ancient mind forgets.

To Philippina

Lady fair, lady fair,
Seated with the scornful,
Though your beauty be so rare,
I were but a born fool
Still to seek my pleasure there.

To love your features and your hue,
All your glowing beauty,

All, in short, that's good of you,
Was and is my duty,
As to love all beauty too.

But now a fairer face I've got,
A Picture's—and believe me,
I never looked to you for what
A picture cannot give me.
All you've more, enhances not.

Your queenly lips can speak, and prove
The means of your uncrowning;
Your brow can change, your eyes can move,
Which grants you power of frowning;
Hers have Heav'n's one thought, of Love.

So now I give good-bye, ma belle,
And lose no great good by it.
You're fair, well!—I can smile farewell,
As you must shortly sigh it,
To your bright, light, outer shell.

Wayside Flowers

Pluck not the wayside flower,
It is the traveller's dower;
A thousand passers-by
Its beauties may espy,
May win a touch of blessing
From Nature's mild caressing.

William Allingham

The sad of heart perceives
A violet under leaves

Like sonic fresh-budding hope;
The primrose on the slope
A spot of sunshine dwells,
And cheerful message tells
Of kind renewing power;
The nodding bluebell's dye
Is drawn from happy sky.
Then spare the wayside flower!
It is the traveller's dower.

The Western Wind

The Western Wind blows free and far
Under the lonely Evening Star
Across an ocean vague and vast,
And sweeps that Island Bay at last;
Blows over cliff there, over sand,
Over mountain-guarded land,
Rocky pastures, moors and lakes,
Rushing River that forsakes
His inland calm to find the tide;
Homes where Men in turn abide;

And blows into my heart with thrills,
Remembered thrills of love and joy.
I see thee, Star, above the hills
And waves, as tho' again a Boy,

And yet through mist of tears.
O shine In other hearts, as once in mine,
And thou, Atlantic Wind, blow free
For others now, as once for me !

Writing

A man who keeps a diary, pays
Due toll to many tedious days;
But life becomes eventful--then
His busy hand forgets the pen.
Most books, indeed, are records less
Of fulness than of emptiness.

Made in the USA
Las Vegas, NV
04 February 2025

17551557R00049